PORTRAIT OF A PHYSICIAN. *School of ʿAqā Riżā.*

PERSIAN PAINTING

Persian Painting

BY

BASIL GRAY

ASSISTANT KEEPER
IN THE
BRITISH MUSEUM

LONDON

Ernest Benn, Limited

Bouverie House, Fleet Street, E.C. 4

Printed
in
Great Britain

First Impression December 1930
Second Impression December 1930

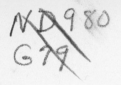
PREFACE

I HAVE tried in this short book to give an introduction to the study of Persian painting. My object has been, in the first place, to show how very well worth looking at are these Persian miniatures, and then to provide some guidance among the succession of schools. In writing it I have thought not only of the several big volumes containing reproductions of these paintings, to which reference has been made in the text; but also of the unrivalled opportunity, provided by the International Persian Exhibition at Burlington House, of seeing them in their actual glowing colours. In the historical treatment I hope I have not seemed to attach too great an importance to dating: it is often hazardous and seldom quite certain; and, with a people so conservative and archaistic as the Persians, perhaps not very important. But there is a freshness in the first treatment of any design which makes it particularly charming, as well as of value for the disentangling of origins. So that precedence is of some moment. Incidentally, I have silently changed all dates throughout the book to the Christian equivalent, to the nearest year, of the actual figures in the manuscripts, which are reckoned on the Mohammedan system.

If I have avoided any direct comparison with European painters, it is because it does not seem to serve any useful purpose to detect resemblances in general character between artists of two schools whose aims were so different, and not because I do not think the Persian school comparable in quality. In their own line of decoration the Persians scored successes more often and more easily than the painters of Europe in theirs. They are less likely nowadays to be accused of shirking the difficulties of anatomy and chiaroscuro.

The illustrations have all been chosen from English collections, both because the originals are always comparatively accessible, and because up to the present they have not been accorded sufficient prominence in general books on the subject. Although there is a shortage of private collectors in this country, it will be seen, when the catalogue of Mr. Chester Beatty's collection is published, that there is one equal to anything in Paris, and if the public collections in the British Museum, the India Office and the Bodleian Library are considered, it will be realised that this country is actually not at all poorer than France. I am indebted to Dr. Barnett,

Keeper of Oriental Books and Manuscripts at the British Museum, and to Dr. Cowley, Bodley's Librarian, for facilities to photograph manuscripts under their care, and for leave to reproduce from them. To the President and Council of the Royal Asiatic Society I am particularly indebted for leave to reproduce, for the first time, a page from their magnificent *Shāh-nāma*, which the Society hope to publish shortly *in extenso*. Finally, to my colleague, Mr. J. V. S. Wilkinson, I am much indebted for constant help and encouragement.

The Bibliography is intended to indicate means for pursuing the study of Persian painting, mainly through reproductions. It is clearly not exhaustive; and while the author is indebted to all those sources, he would record especial obligation to Dr. Martin's great book, which was the pioneer general treatment of the subject but which remains indispensable, and to the work of Sir Thomas Arnold. He had thrown much light on the subject matter of Islamic painting and its origins, through his unrivalled knowledge of the native sources. He showed iconography to be not academic but the root of the whole matter. His death is an irreparable loss to the study of Islamic art.

B. G.

September 1930.

LEADING DATES

CONTENTS

xi

LIST OF THE PLATES

PERSIAN PAINTING

CHAPTER I

PERSIAN ART AND PERSIAN HISTORY

A N Y O N E who has ever seen any piece of Persian stuff, any tile or mirror-back, must at once have felt that the Persians are the great designers of the world. The glories of Persian carpets are well known, but their appreciation is perhaps more abstruse. It is in colour and balance that a design shows its excellence; and in both the Persians are masters. They have always used the best and purest colours with masterly effect, and have never been afraid of the repeat pattern that is so restful and satisfying to the eye. Probably the Persians drew many motives from the great pool of primitive art which came ultimately from the plains of Central Asia. The most conspicuous elements of this early art were animal forms and geometric patterns. The earliest specimens of Persian art were of this kind, Sasanian stuffs and metal-work.

15

For there is a cultural and political gap between Sasanian
Persia and the old Achæmenid kingdom: in later days
the Sasanian period is a living memory in the national
conscience; the Achæmenids are a misunderstood legend.
Their monuments may have influenced later art, but
externally and no more than the Assyrians. But from
Sasanian times onwards there is a real unity in Persian
art, which is always conservative, with a consistent
development of the early decorative ideas.   The Sasanian
bronze-work is the finest of its kind, and the stuffs of
this period, though probably owing something to Coptic
Egypt in technique and organisation, show great strength
in their pigments. Of those which have survived,
mostly protected in the precious reliquaries of Christian
cathedrals, the most important collection is in Berlin.
Their most notable invention is that of confrontation of
warriors, horsemen, heads of horses and of cocks. This
type of design was adopted in the workshops of Byzantium
and from there exported to every part of Europe.[1]

This Persian instinct for balance, ranging from simple
confrontation to elaborate compositions, and for colour

[1] For reproductions of some of these designs see *Revue des Arts
Asiatiques*, tom. vi. no. 1; *Annales du Musée Guimet*, tom. 5, Les
Portraits d'Antinoé.

persists: none of the invasions of unparalleled violence, Mohammedan, Mongol, Timurid, destroyed it. The nation is constantly returning for strength and inspiration to the Sasanian age: witness the great epic, the most popular book in Persia, the " Shāh-nāma," or Book of Kings, which was the versified history of early Persia, produced by Firdausī to the order of one of the conquering princes. Only slightly less popular than this work was that of Nizāmī, who also dealt with a few of the most picturesque stories of the heroic period. Indeed these became the regular stock in trade of all writers of epic. As at Athens, the poets rivalled one another in perpetual treatment of the same themes. So too even in painting there is evidence that a good deal survived down to the tenth or eleventh century which has since completely vanished. Judging from the fragments of Manichæan manuscripts that have survived, it was close to the earliest specimens that we possess of the Islamic period in Persia.

The main result of the forcible conversion of Persia to the faith of Islām has been to thwart the essentially artistic instincts of the race. Wherever possible, in tiles and carpets and coloured stucco in the mosques and medressehs, the Persians, followed by the Turks, have lavished colour. But in spite of the nationalist character of the Shī'ite heresy in Persia, which was very marked, there was nothing doctrinal in this "reformation." Objection to the portrayal of the human form, an old Semitic tenet, remained. Consequently the religion of the Persians, by which, too, all education was controlled, has never developed to the full the artistic qualities of the race. But thanks to the Arab conquest Persia was for a time part of a large empire from which she derived much of permanent value, and not least the Arabic script.

But with the Mongol invasions the international quality of her civilisation stops gradually. Mesopotamia was for a time still included and Baghdad remained a centre of culture, though sadly fallen from its old position; manuscripts were produced there in the full Persian style throughout the fourteenth century. But though the Mongol Ilkhans adopted the Mohammedan religion without reservation, that did not prevent a complete enmity with the Mamluk sultans even in the face of a non-Moslem enemy. The Mongol and Timurid invaders had no art of their own to force on the country they had conquered. The civilisation of Turkestan had long since receded towards China. But they did open up closer communications

with the East: at the Timurid court nothing was valued
so highly as a Chinese painting.   But so far back as the
time of Firdausī (eleventh century), " Chinese " was used
as equivalent to " Parisian."   The Timurids were more
civilised, by contact with the Persians, at the time of their
invasions: they had reached the stage of wanting the
best art that money could buy.   This snobbishness led
to a rivalry between the various princes to gather at
their courts as many artists and men of science as possible.
Even Tīmūr himself, though, as we see him through the
eyes of the Spanish ambassador Clavijo, he preferred
living the nomad life surrounded by his horde and gorging
himself at endless feasts, set about the building of mosques
and colleges at his new capital of Samarqand.   But
Persia has never really recovered from these invasions
and the internecine struggles of her ruling families.
Money was increasingly in the hands of the ruling class,
which till the rise of the Safavids was foreign.   But it is
a curious fact that the great period of Persian culture is
under these foreign dynasties, and that with the national
dynasty decadence soon set it.   Perhaps the explanation
is that while there was sufficient energy in the country,
art and strife continued, but that later with exhaustion
came unity and decadence.

CHAPTER II

THE POSITION OF PAINTING IN PERSIA

PAINTING in Persia thus started under an immense disadvantage. In practically every other country painting has grown up as a servant of religion. The effect of this, at least at first, has not been to hamper its development, but rather to provide the artist with work for a purpose to which he was enthusiastically devoted. The preservation of continuity by some organised body such as a church, which might impose those conventions that are so useful to a young art, was lacking. Iconographic conventions governed the productions of the triumphs of early Buddhist and Byzantine painting. It was only when they became too stringent that the effect was deadening. Persian painting was popularly supposed to have had its origin in just such a religious system, Manichæanism, which made great use of it liturgically, and which in its eclecticism was so typical of the Persian attitude. Yet it was violently persecuted; its founder, Mani, the first Persian artist, was killed in A.D. 290 and its illuminated books were burned. Yet it survived for centuries, and must have exercised in fact some influence on the origin of Persian miniature painting.

But with the Mohammedan conquest the field of painting was permanently limited. Banned by the religion of the country, representational art was confined to the palaces of the great: painting in Persia was never in any sense popular. The painters of Persia were humble servants in aristocratic households. At most periods artists have been primarily craftsmen, but in Persia their work was only a fresco in a bath-room or an illustration to a volume of history or poetry, both out of the view of the ordinary man. There was little incentive in subject or critic to good work; and yet the romantic illustrative style of the work was equally suited to the character of the people and the purpose of the painting.

So it would seem unreasonable to claim with Dr. Martin a central position for painting among the arts in Persia, and to attribute to the miniature painter the origination of the designs appearing in textiles and ceramics. This may possibly have been the position in the early Safavid period, when art of all sorts was the monopoly of the aristocracy, but it is impossible to believe that the designs on the pottery of " Rhages " ware were derived from the miniature painters of the day. Both surely had a common parentage. Dr. Martin wrote at a time when enthusiasm for the recently " discovered " Persian miniature painting was roused to its highest point after the exhibitions at Munich in 1910 and Paris in 1912. In correcting a previous neglect it not unnaturally erred on the side of exaggeration. But it is possible to make out a very strong case absolutely for Persian painting. In the field to which it was restricted, partly by circumstances, it attained very near to perfection in its masterpieces and to such a high general standard that scarcely any Persian miniature fails to charm. This is partly due to the exquisite enamelled effect produced by the colours that the miniature painters used: for, whereas practically all dyes used in Persian carpets are vegetable, which never perish the wool or silk, so practically all the paints are mineral and suffer scarcely at all from fading, and unless attacked by damp are very permanent. This is particularly true of the pure colours, white made from white-lead, black from lamp-black, ochres yellow and brown, made from the clay of Hormuz or Multan, and above all the famous lapis-lazuli blue. By the time of the Safavids a new deeper blue was introduced to the Eastern world through the conquest of Hungary by the

Turks, which gave access to a supply of azurite. Green
was always rather a difficult colour: the two commonest
preparations were made from a mixture of orpiment, a
metallic arsenic, and indigo, and from verdigris. A
glowing rose was made by mixing white-lead from
Kashgar and vermilion (sulphide of mercury). In addition, both gold and silver were freely used: the former
in leaf for the sky, for which it served indifferently as an
alternative to blue at all periods, and in solution for
painting borders and details. The silver, in later periods
only used for representing water, has of course oxidised.
But this is the one serious chemical change which has
befallen the miniatures.

Such a palette demanded a wealthy patron, and not
less expensive was the paper which was so carefully prepared and polished. Rag paper was introduced from
China to Samarqand in A.D. 751, and the industry
remained established there for centuries. Already by the
tenth century there were several sorts in existence, and
the varieties steadily increased. The most expensive
sort was the rather thick paper covered with gold-dust,
which was extensively used about 1500. For calligraphy
and for painting the paper was polished with an egg-
shaped crystal and sometimes afterwards with soap.

Sketches were first made on poorer paper and then traced on this prepared surface by means of a pricked gazelle skin. The outline was then drawn in various coloured inks, the commonest being sanguine and indigo, both of which are used in the drawing reproduced on Plate 10. Then the colours were filled in, working from the lighter to the darker shades. Sometimes details such as moustaches and beards seem to have been added last after the paint, but the folds in drapery are usually represented by drawing under the paint, which is, of course, absolutely clear. Finally, the miniature was marginated with three or four distinct bands. Occasionally the border would be illuminated in the same way as the unvāns or headings of the text of the manuscript.

Such extreme care in execution and such brilliant, clear and costly materials naturally produce an exquisite effect. But the glory of Persian miniature painting is the marvellously sensitive sinuous line and the fineness of detail with an inexhaustible fertility of invention, at any rate in the best period. It is possible that Persian miniatures may at first appear somewhat monotonous. Apart from the fatigue to the unaccustomed eye of looking at such bright colours and such fine detail, a greater similarity may seem to persist through Persian miniatures because of certain omissions and certain conventions. Like all Eastern artists, the Persian never drew shadow or reflection: to do so would be to emphasise too much the point of view of the artist. Then he is more inventive in subject than experimental in method. He will thus usually represent horses broad side on, though in certain polo and battle scenes horses are viewed directly from behind. Again, in these miniatures practically all the faces are seen three-quarters, with a single line indicating the outline from one ear to the opposite eye-socket. In fact the artists are not very interested in figure-drawing. There are, it is true, those many single figures of the later period, but the interest is rather in the line of the drapery than in anything else. Certainly no artist has had more attractive clothes on his models. So the figure is not much indicated; even the feet and hands are frequently covered, while the body is rather elongated to show to advantage the line of the long coat. As practically the only difference between male and female costume was in the head-dress, the scenes appear rather peopled with dummies without sex or personality. Profiles are rare in these scenes from a golden age where all are youthful, but in exceptional cases, where the subjects require the introduction of an old beggar-woman, the contrast is all the greater. This same type constantly recurs. Finally, all these scenes are laid in bright spring sunshine: the fruit trees are always in flower, and if the trees are sometimes bare of leaves, it is clearly a fortunate accident permitting one the better to appreciate the shapes of their branches. But there is really no end to the variety of treatment of these scenes, each one filled with so many objects that charm the eye. In fact the artist is all the time achieving the exact object he had in view. It was the external conditions, political and social, that prevented painting in Persia from developing beyond this position: it remained at the first stage of the renaissance, showing intense delight in the physical world and in the mastery of its own technique. Up to 1400 Persian painting developed almost parallel with Western Europe. One can only regret the chance that made further progress impossible.

CHAPTER III

THE INTERNATIONAL ABBASID SCHOOL

A L T H O U G H it is known that the Sasanian palaces were decorated with paintings, nothing is known to have survived to show what they were like. Sir Thomas Arnold [1] has drawn attention to what evidence there is— mostly drawn from silver-work—to prove the surviving influence of Sasanian art in Persian painting. He has also somewhat enlarged on Von le Coq's [2] suggestion that the fragments of Manichæan manuscripts found by him at Chotscho, and now in Berlin, indicate an art which must have flourished for four hundred years and survived in Turkestan up to 1036, when Chotscho was destroyed, thus overlapping the beginnings of illumination in Persia under Islamic rule. He mainly emphasised the iconographic peculiarities of certain representations of Christian subjects in Arabic manuscripts, only to be

[1] " Survivals in Persian Painting," Oxford, 1924.
[2] " Chotscho," 1913, Pls. 1–6; " Die manichæschen Miniaturen," 1923.

explained by the supposition of an origin in the hybrid
system of the Manichæans. But more significant is the
colouring, with a marked preference for blue—Von le
Coq calls it a true ultramarine—and in the patterns on
the robes, which are just those squares and rosettes which
recur in Arabic and Persian manuscripts for centuries.
They probably come from China by way of Turkestan,
as the finely indicated priests' robes certainly do. It is
interesting to see a very close parallel to these Manichæan
priests as late as 1511 in a manuscript of Nizāmī at the
Bodleian Library (Elliott 192, fol. 115b), where there is
a miniature showing the Ka'ba.

But the study of Persian painting starts with the
manuscripts of the Abbasid period. " Abbasid School "
or " Mesopotamian " is the name given to the whole
bulk of illuminated manuscripts produced while the
Abbasid Caliphs reigned in their luxurious capital at
Baghdad (750–1258). If it is a mistake to look upon
this art as Arab, it is equally a mistake to consider it
Persian. It is true that the Persians were the only one
of the peoples among whom it flourished to develop
anything from it: in Spain it remained crystallised for
centuries; a debased form survives in North Africa; in
Egypt religious scruples were sufficiently strong to prevent

the rise of a miniature school in the great period of Islamic art under the Fatimids. But there can be no question that the predominant formative influence is that of the adherents of the Christian churches in the East. They probably furnished most of the artists at Baghdad, as they certainly did practically all the craftsmen of Damascus and Aleppo, where they introduced the glories of Byzantine mosaic work in the eighth century. It is also worth noting that Christians were responsible for the work of translating the classical authors into Arabic. Sir Thomas Arnold, in " Painting in Islam," has worked out some interesting iconographic parallels between Christian, Syriac and Arabic manuscripts, and he particularly suggests a strong Nestorian influence and the possibility of borrowing from the anomalous city of Harran, which remained heathen till the thirteenth century.

There is no wish to depreciate the great qualities of Islamic civilisation, which preserved so much of classical culture and presented it to Europe, and which for six hundred years united the Near East and enabled ideas to be exchanged freely from Cordova to Samarqand. But the Arabs were not great originators nor great artists. If their early craftsmen and scholars were mostly

3

Christian, there is plenty of evidence to show that at Baghdad by the twelfth century they were mainly Persian —to the disgust of the Arabs.   But it was the Arab power that brought together those varied influences from East Christians, Persians, and probably not least from Coptic Egypt, which fused into Islamic art.

Painting, which had first appeared in the bathrooms of the great, was in demand during this period for the illustration of two classes of books.   There were certain scientific treatises on medicine, astronomy and physics to which illustrations were a necessary supplement. As integral features of the manuscript these naturally survived many copyings over a long period with only minor changes.   So that although none of the known illuminated manuscripts are earlier than the twelfth century, they must in some cases, such as those of Dioscorides, preserve pretty faithfully the work of several centuries earlier. Among these the most notable are the manuscripts containing zodiacal figures, and certain treatises on hydraulics, the most famous of which is a copy of al-Jazari's book on mechanical contrivances written in Syria in 1180.   This copy is in the library of St. Sophia at Constantinople, but certain leaves removed from it were exhibited at the Munich Exhibition of 1910, though they have only

1. CLEPSYDRA.

recently been identified by Professor Riefstahl.[1] It was written in Egypt in 1354. Another copy of this manuscript has been in the Bodleian Library, where it is Greaves No. 27, since the seventeenth century. Plate 1 shows a diagram of a water clock which gives some idea of the decorative effect of these strictly scientific manuscripts. The colouring is in a plain wash, with a good deal of yellow. This copy was made in 1496, but according to the colophon from a version of 1341.

The most famous of all these scientific manuscripts is a Dioscorides dated 1222 and now dispersed. It is a very splendid manuscript, the pages being beautifully balanced and enriched with gold. The colour-scheme is attractive, if subdued: a fine pale blue and indigo contrast with touches of dull crimson. It is notable that while the plants in this and the Qazwīnī manuscripts are very similar to those in Greek herbals and the original Dioscorides, the figures both in colouring and the pattern of their clothes, in design and colouring, recall the Manichæan paintings, though the shading in both is rather near to the representations in Byzantine mosaics.

Such scientific manuscripts as this must have been executed for wealthy patrons: very different is the other

[1] In *The Art Bulletin*, Vol. XI. no. 2. New York, June, 1929.

class which employed the artist.   Two of the most popular
Arabic books which became classics soon after they were
written were the " Kalīla wa Dimna " of Ibnu'l Muqaffa,
who died about A.D. 760, and the " Maqāmāt " of Harīrī
(1054–1122).   The former was a translation of the Pehlevi
version of the Sanskrit " Fables of Bidpai," animal fables
which have appeared in most European and Asiatic
languages during their long life.   The " Maqāmāt " or
" Assemblies " of Harīrī is a rhyming prose work—the
Canterbury Tales of the Arab—in which a certain Abu
Zayd displays his craftiness in a series of adventures,
some edifying and some the reverse.   It was written at
the instance of a Persian statesman living in retirement
at Basra, and some of the scenes are laid in Persia.   So
that both these popular books had a particular connection
with Persia.   The copies that have survived, mostly in a
fragmentary condition, vary in quality, but they are all
emphatically plain books.   Even the most important
manuscript in the Bibliothèque Nationale, known from
its former owner as the Schefer Harīrī, is not a luxurious
book.   The drawings are full of vigour, the pen being
vigorously wielded in discursive strokes.   The colouring
is rather crude and the palette limited: these are illustrative drawings and not true miniatures.   It will be
noted that in all the manuscripts of this Abbasid school

the illustrations are not marked off from the rest of the page. They are part of the text, rather than opportunities for artistic effort. But the characterisation is splendid: it has been said that the Schefer Harīrī is a vivid portrayal of Arabic life: so too animals have never been drawn with greater sympathy than in these fable books. One of the earliest known copies of this book, dated 1180, is at Paris: it corresponds very closely with another manuscript in the Bodleian Library, which may belong to the following century. Plate 2 shows a fight between the lion and the elephant. The indication of hair with a few economical strokes is typical of these miniatures, and the lion's head comes straight out of a Sasanian material at the same remove as the tiger and camel on the coronation robe in the Schatz Kammer at Vienna. Both features were extensively copied in later Persian miniatures.

In the manuscript of Dioscorides it was natural to find Classical influence, but there is also very considerable Byzantine influence to be traced in this popular style. The drapery hangs in the same highly conventionalised heavy folds, and the actual arrangement of the figures is sometimes traceable to a Christian source. The round halo is freely used to give importance to any particular person, or merely as a background for the heads of men,

and sometimes even of birds.   But this is not necessarily
a sign of Christian influence.   Then the background or
setting which is inevitable as a stage property, probably
out of the common primitive " horreur de vide," is
always borrowed from Christian manuscripts.   The two
common forms are the architectural and the vegetable.
As in the Rabula Gospels, trees grow as if flattened for a
collector's cabinet with a few leaves arranged on either
side; occasional small plants sprout underfoot.   If the
classical pillars have been whittled away, the architrave
they support is very close to such representations as in
the Etschmiadzin Gospels.   It is curious to see the frame
of a canon table once more serving an architectural
purpose.   Possibly some of the resemblances to Byzantine
work in the manuscripts of this international Abbasid
style may be due to independent borrowing from Sasanian
art as it is in textiles, but it is reasonable to expect some
Byzantine influence, considering what very great opportunities it had of forming this new art.

It has been suggested that some of these manuscripts
may have been produced at Ghazna, a Persian city in
what is now Afghanistan, where Sultān Mahmūd (998–
1030) and a short line of diminishing importance held
their court till they were finally extinguished in 1186.

2. LION AND ELEPHANT FIGHTING.

Mahmūd, though the son of a slave's slave, was a great conqueror and wished to appear a great patron. He compelled distinguished savants to come to his capital: the chronologer al-Bīrūnī had to submit, but the great doctor Avicenna succeeded in escaping on the way. But his most important work in his Persian national revival was his commissioning of Firdausī to produce an epic on the ancient history of the Persian kings. He wrote his historical poem in a room decorated with paintings, we are told. But there is no evidence that either here or at the other centres of this national revival at Rayy (Teherān), Bukhara or Khiva any different style of art was practised than in Mesopotamia. The power of the Caliphs was on the wane and Persian influence was dominant throughout Iraq as well as Persia. Persian patrons were no more likely to order a new style of manuscript in one place than the other: their religious scruples must have been equally lively in both. There is a story that Sultān Mahmūd himself, hearing that his son had had a pavilion painted with licentious scenes, sent a messenger secretly to find out the truth of the report: the young man received a warning and had the paintings whitewashed over in time. Moreover, the pottery for which Rayy (Rhages) is famous, and which comes precisely from one of these national centres, is notably similar in style of decoration to the manuscripts of Mesopotamia. The leaves collected in an album in the Serai Library at Stambul, and which M. Sakisian has recently published as, in part, the product of this Ghaznavid school, cannot be considered earlier than the Mongol invasions. Even less probable seems to be Dr. Martin's attribution of a manuscript of Bidpai belonging to Mr. Dyson Perrins to this school. It is dated 1262, but his catalogue, while accepting this date for the text, seems rightly to date the miniatures as fourteenth or early fifteenth work of an archaistic kind.

In short, there can be no distinction between the miniatures produced in Persia during this "international" period and anywhere else in Hither Asia. The only difficulty in the way of considering the Persians as the dominant exponents of this art in its later phases is that of accounting for the violent change in the character of miniature painting in Persia immediately the unity was broken by the Mongol invasions. It apparently required this violent shock to enable the Persian genius to develop a new art on its own lines under the quickening influence of intercourse with the Far East.

CHAPTER IV

TWO TARTAR INVASIONS AND THE FUSING OF A NEW ART

I T is impossible to over-estimate the importance of the Mongol invasions in art any more than in political history. But it is difficult to account for the extraordinarily flourishing state of art and letters under this Tartar dominion, after the wholesale havoc wrought by these barbarians. The fourteenth century is one of the most fruitful periods in the history of Persian poetry: the fourteenth century also witnessed almost the whole evolution of Persian miniature painting. With the Timurids came the period of its highest development, and the same age saw the last of the classic poets, Jāmī. Afterwards, under the Safavids, in spite of material recovery there was no further progress. It seems to be useless merely to say that art flourishes in periods of disturbance. In the present case it looks rather as though the impetus came actually from the previous age, and that painting was ready to develop immediately it was given a powerful

lead; as soon as the patrons really wanted a decorative
work, and not merely an illustrated book. In fact it
needed a revival of the old tradition.[1]

The art of this period is generally described as Mongol,
but this is really rather misleading. Naturally the costumes and the physical types portrayed are those of the
conquering race, and they ride the small Mongol horses.
The tents of the horde become henceforward a prominent
feature in the landscapes, with their bell-shaped tops,
straight sides and richly woven materials. In one of the
miniatures here reproduced (Plate 4) the horsehair plumes
which the Mongol warriors carried just below their lance-
tops may be seen, and so may something else of very
much greater significance; there are two standards
against the skyline, and on one of them as well as on the
breast of a man in the foreground it is possible to make
out a Chinese dragon. Though the invaders were
Mongol, what they brought with them was Chinese:
this is the new element which appears in Persian painting
and which is never afterwards wholly absent again.
Persia now formed part of an empire which extended to
the further side of Asia, and though the political bond

[1] The first trace of this is to be seen in pages from a " Shāh-nāma "
of *c.* 1200 belonging to Mr. Chester Beatty.

was loose and soon parted, trade and diplomatic communications were constant.

But though Chinese influence may be directly traced
in the borrowing of details, it was far more important as
a formative ideal which made the Persian artist realise
the possibilities of his craft. And in fact after the fall of
Baghdad in 1258 miniatures executed in Persia were
more Persian than they had ever been before. Even the
traditional subjects were immediately changed. The
magnificent manuscript of Ibn Bakhtishu's natural
history, now in the Pierpont Morgan Library in New
York, contains many representations of animals such as
might have occurred in a copy of the " Fables of Bidpai."
But how different is the new treatment! The animals
begin to be treated schematically and with humour. In
them there seems to be a return to the spirit in which
the Sasanian woven stuffs were produced, the queer
patterning on some of the beasts being very similar in
both. At the same time the trees become more leafy,
they begin to bend in the wind and to curl into whirls:
in fact they have become decorative. This manuscript
was produced at Tabriz in 1295. The new centre is not
on the borders of Central Asia, where the Mongol influence
must be supposed to have been strongest, but on the

near side of the Caspian Sea, where perhaps the desolation was less severe.

A little later the famous minister and historian and patron Rashīdu'd-Dīn (1247–1318) built a suburb outside Tabrīz, named after him Rashīdiyya. Here he kept a large staff constantly engaged in copying and illustrating his own works, historical and philosophical, to the composition of which he devoted every moment when he was not transacting public business. Fortunately there is in existence the greater part of a manuscript produced in this studio. It is a copy of Rashīdu'd-Dīn's " History of the World," dated 1306–12, and of which some sixty leaves are preserved by the Royal Asiatic Society, and 277 pages are at the Edinburgh University library. This manuscript is of the greatest importance as giving an idea of the state of Persian painting at this time and for disentangling the various strands of influence which were not yet inextricably twisted into the stuff of Persian art. Some of the miniatures illustrate Biblical subjects such as Jonah and the whale, others scenes from the life of Mohammed, others again Buddhist scenes laid in India. The second part, which was the first written, is a History of the Mongols, and in this Chinese influence is more marked. Continental critics have been disturbed by this

3. Mongols in Armour.

manuscript, which they have regarded as a freak, because
it does not fit in with their scheme of the development
of the Persian art style. But if it is taken as a starting-
point there is less difficulty about it; it is easy to find
parallels to almost every feature of it in later manuscripts.
The Christian part, it is generally agreed, must have
been derived from an illuminated Bible—Sir T. Arnold
has suggested Nestorian. It seems unlikely that different
artists worked exclusively at these: though more than
one hand is traceable, they cannot be distinguished thus
according to subject. On the other hand, it is quite
possible that there were Chinese artists in Rashīdu'd-
Dīn's studio capable of displaying and explaining the
Chinese style. Certainly the direct Chinese influence in
detail is greater here than it ever was again; and it is
known that Rashīdu'd-Dīn had Chinese to help him with
his history. No doubt some sort of unity was imposed
on the work of the school by a head of the department.

The landscape, and especially the mountains, is rather
reminiscent of T'ang painting, but the way the figures
are set on the paper is quite unChinese. As will be seen
from Plate 3, the grouping is clumsy, though the gestures
are expressive and seem to be the successors of the gestures
in the Abbasid Harīrī manuscripts. The hands are rather

similar in drawing and nothing like them occurs later. The shadows are put in with silver that has since oxidised, and the long heavy folds are a curious mixture of the sensitive Chinese line and the hieratic stiffness which the Abbasid school received from Byzantium. The armour is of the scaly plated sort which the Mongols carried across Asia and which survived in Japan. The drawing of the skirts is in red, and further red is introduced in the spear shafts and the saddles. These long-shaped miniatures seem particularly well-suited to the big pages of calligraphy, and they have a bigness about them which has led some people to think that they may be copied from wall-paintings; but for this there is no evidence.

Rashīdu'd-Dīn was disgraced and executed in 1318, as the result of an intrigue; and his suburb with all its library was afterwards destroyed. But, as for five years his works had been copied there, there must have been a number of copies distributed by then to various cities according to his plan. It is true that the work is rare, but there is no need to assume, in defiance of stylistic evidence, that the fine undated manuscript in the Bibliothèque Nationale must have been executed before 1318. There are plenty of dated manuscripts coming from the middle of the fourteenth century in spite of the anarchy then prevailing in Persia, and this manuscript should be assigned to the period of about 1340 to 1350.

The bulk of these manuscripts are new versions of the Arabic classics, their illumination growing freer and freer in treatment and more decorative though less vigorous. But there is also a magnificent copy of Firdausī's great epic, the Book of Kings, which used to belong to M. Demotte and was dated by him 1310. It is now dispersed among many collections, several sheets being in Paris and the rest in America. Stylistically this shows a considerable development from the Edinburgh and R.A.S. manuscript. The horses are very similar and so is the landscape: the heavy Byzantine folds and the looped-up curtains still occur here, especially in the throne scenes, but the elaborate throne structures seem derived from the Egyptian illuminations, from which the Byzantines also borrowed architectural frames for their canon tables. Even more interesting is the appearance of certain motives which recur throughout the history of Persian miniature painting. The Chinese cloud has become more formalised, though it is not quite so solid or so simple as it became later. But in the divan scenes and the scene of Zāl and Rūdābah appear two of the commonest designs in Persian painting. In the former the main figure is roughly central, the minor persons arranged in a fan shape below him; at the back trees appear as relief in the corner on either side. In the latter the wall of a house occupies the whole of one side of the composition, while the other, in which the figures are placed, is by contrast full of luxuriant vegetation. In fact there is a definite system of planes: the high horizon is appearing. In the R.A.S. manuscript the mountains had simply formed a background like a drop-scene; they were henceforward used as a convenient aid to the arrangement of elaborate compositions. In this manuscript too appears an illustration of the famous story of Bahram Gūr and his mistress, the design for which seems directly derived from a well-known Sasanian design, an example of which is on a silver dish in the Hermitage Museum. They were out hunting together and she set him the task of pinning with an arrow the hind hoof of a gazelle to its ear. He accomplishes it by first tickling the ear with one arrow and then pinning the hoof to it with another as the animal raises it to scratch itself in flight. As in most copies of this long work the miniatures are of uneven quality, but judging from the general style it seems to belong to about 1330.

In the Bibliothèque Nationale manuscript of the

" History of the Mongols " mentioned above the decorative character is much more pronounced. The artist has begun to insert single plants carefully painted wherever he found room, and the plane tree with its multicoloured leaves so dear to the Persian makes its first appearance. So too does the habit of forming the rocks into fantastic animal heads, which survived on into Mughal art. The tents are covered with arabesque and floral patterns of considerable complexity. There is still a tendency to group the figures together in bunches, and the colouring is not particularly pleasing. There are yellows and browns which give the whole a rather muddy appearance and the composition is often clumsy. But the manuscript is a document of first-rate importance for the state of miniature painting about 1350.

Between 1381 and 1392 occurred the invasions of Tamerlane, with even greater holocausts than accompanied the first Tartar wave; indeed he seems to have been quite definitely a victim of blood-lust. But there was also a renewal of Chinese influence. Tīmūr set about gathering at Samarqand as many skilled craftsmen as possible from each town that he captured; so that there was never any risk of a break in the continuity of development of style. And Tīmūr himself and his whole family

4

seem to have been professed patrons of the arts. Tīmūr
must have been an awkward person to work for; it is
related that once when he went to look at the great
mosque that was being built to his order and glory at
Samarqand, he found the door too low. The whole was
pulled down and rebuilt within a week, so great was his
impatience and the terror he inspired. There is no
evidence that he ever patronised miniature painters:
very likely he was too strict a Moslem, like many converts,
and in any case he was illiterate. His successor, Shāh
Rukh (1404–1447), and his sons were very good patrons
of painters.

Throughout this period intercourse with China was
pretty close, so that it is not surprising to find scenes like
one in the Bibliothèque Nationale " History of the
Mongols " (Martin: Pl. 43) representing a court pro-
cession, which is put on the page in a very Chinese way,
strongly reminiscent of a Yuan makimono. Very different,
though even more directly taken from a Chinese painting,
is a well-known picture on silk in the Goloubew collection,
now in the Museum of Fine Arts, Boston, in which a
blue bird perches on a bough of camelia, manifestly of
Ming origin. This is probably about a century later in
date. Chinese influence was evidently constantly at work

and must be assumed to have been the formative influence
throughout this period; though it is difficult always to
see exactly its working. But the steadily improving
organisation of the miniatures must owe a good deal to
its example. Another notable characteristic is the ever
more decorative nature of the work. While naturalistic
drawing of details is increasing, the page is arranged in
an ever more arbitrary way, trees and mountains, clouds
and plants are all called in to make as effective a whole
as possible. It is perhaps in the free draughtsmanship
that Chinese influence is most valuable. Both races are
great calligraphers, and for both painting is closely connected with calligraphy. The minute detail of the
Persian miniature is a natural concomitant of the exquisite
fineness and steadiness of Persian writing, just as the
broad line of the Chinese character which only an artist
can form well is to be seen in the great ink landscapes of
the Sung school. In both, too, artistic effect is the chief
aim, the illustrative side being so secondary that the
main character or action is as easily overlooked in Persian
(cf. Martin, Pl. 50; Kühnel, Pl. 42) as in Chinese paintings. Perhaps the parallel ends here; for in each case
the artist has claimed a free hand for his own purpose;
the Chinese for spiritual or emotional expression, the

Persian for a supremely decorative effect, full of every delight which he could imagine.

These tendencies are well seen as early as the end of the fourteenth century in two manuscripts in the British Museum. The first is a copy of three poems by Khwaju of Kirman (1281–*c.* 1350), written at Baghdad in 1397. Of the nine miniatures, six were reproduced by Dr. Martin (Pls. 45–50); and of these, three have been republished elsewhere, so that the manuscript is well known. The second, which is of the same date, contains several poems, each of which has a marvellous frontispiece sarlauhs and unvāns decorated in turquoise blue and gold. One is a copy of a rare ryhmed history, by Ahmad of Tabrīz, of the conquests of Chingīz Khan, the King of kings (see Plate 4).

These early Timurid miniatures are much more spacious than anything that had gone before. This effect is helped by a true bird's-eye perspective, more consistently used than it was later, though it was never quite so thoroughly applied to buildings as it was to landscape. At all periods the sheer property wall was a possibility. There is no longer a flat drop-curtain in these miniatures, but figures appear on many different planes and the natural scenery plays an equally prominent

4. THE WARS OF CHINGĪZ KHAN

part in the whole. This tendency is most fully developed
by about 1430, as, for instance, in a well-known miniature
at Leipzig (Kühnel, Pl. 43). In the Khwaju manuscript
there is a remarkable effect of recession, and a further
interesting point is that the miniature is rounded off and
sometimes quite surrounded with trees. The eye is
carried right round the design and brought to rest on the
principal incident in the centre. So, in the page reproduced from the Shāhanshāh Nāma (Plate 4), the composition is equally arranged: the crouching figure at the
bottom is the point on which the eye rests. The battle
is indicated with the greatest economy and without over-
crowding, and yet there is an impression of a big scale,
notably by means of the device of banners carried by
invisible hands behind the rocks against the skyline. In
the bigger Khwaju manuscript the colouring, though
most interesting and gay with its blues and reds, is not
altogether satisfactory: there seems to be rather too
much yellow in the green, though this may be due to
the fading of this notoriously volatile colour; and, besides,
there seems rather too wide a palette, so that the effect
is spotty. But in the smaller Shāhanshāh manuscript
the rocky masses pull the whole colour-scheme together.
The foreground on either side is mauve and the more

distant hills green or peacock blue. The man in the foreground is in dull purple, the other figures and the horses in gold armour with such red and green pattern on it as in the R.A.S. manuscript. The sky is golden. The whole produces an impression of splendour only part of which unfortunately can be conveyed in the plate. It is extraordinary how much progress has been made since the " History of the World " of 1312!

There is a manuscript of about this time which sums up the position rather well and indicates which influences will be likely to be strong enough to survive into the succeeding age, which profited by all the experiments of this period. This is a manuscript which was in the collection of Mr. Yates Thompson and now belongs to M. Gulbenkian. It is dated 1410 and was written for Sultān Iskandar, grandson of Tīmūr, who fell into disgrace two years later, but was then governor of Shīrāz, so that the manuscript may reasonably be attributed to that centre. It contains a number of different works and was evidently illuminated by several different hands: Shīrāz, like Baghdad, can hardly have been stripped of all its best craftsmen to go to Samarqand or Herat, whither Shāh Rukh had transferred his capital. Some of the pages of this manuscript might have been illuminated in

1350, others are in a style that was still in use up to
1500. There are leaves very like the Bibliothèque
Nationale "History of the Mongols"; there are others,
like one of the battle of the clans of Layla and Majnūn,
which might be of any date in the fifteenth century.
The most unusual and interesting of the miniatures are
those illustrating the "Tarīkh i-Guzīda," or Select
History, of Hamdu'llah Mustawfi of Qazwīn. There are
pictures of Adam and Eve naked except for loin-cloths
of leaves, and of the sacrifice of Isaac with what looks
like a calf proffered by the angel. These figures are so
unusually large, though set in a landscape like that of
the Shāhanshāh-nāma, that they must represent, even
so late as this, borrowing from a Nestorian source. The
Aryan types cannot be, as has been suggested, due to
contemporary European influence. But the most typical
of the period are a series of miniatures, slightly more
developed in style than in the two manuscripts of 1396,
and of which another notable example was recently
acquired by the Kaiser Friedrich Museum in Berlin.
This is an Anthology dated 1420, and was also executed
at Shīrāz. In both the figures are rather tall and very
supple: they are on rather a large scale and the horses
are remarkably vigorously drawn. The draperies hang

in slightly heavy folds and the whole treatment is distinctly broad. The same characteristics are to be found in a Shāh-nāma in the Bibliothèque Nationale dated 1430, and in another in the Bodleian Library which cannot be much later, though Sir T. Arnold published a page from it as late fifteenth century.

This is the particular style of the early Timurid period; though it is the smaller scale drawing, represented at this period by the Iskandar-nāma in the British Museum (Add. 27, 261) which was destined to survive the longest. But it was not confined to Herat: though provincial places are certainly apt to preserve outworn fashions, it would be strange if the style of the manuscript that was executed for Baysunqur at Herat or Astarabad should differ widely from that done for his brother at Shirāz. These two styles have been too sharply distinguished: both are to be found in M. Gulbenkian's manuscript. Perhaps Baysunqur had the better taste and realised that the small-scale figures are better suited to the miniature. The style of painting is not so different, the compositions are similar. But with this discovery of the true miniature style the experimental age in the progress of Persian painting is over.

CHAPTER V

MATURITY

S H ā H R u k H died in 1447 and there followed a period
of confusion as great as that of a hundred years before.
But the confusion is perhaps greater for the historian of
the period than it was at the time. Princes constantly
make meteoric appearances; perhaps the country did
not suffer so much after all from their wars. Trade in
1444 from Hormuz was world-wide, regular diplomatic
relations were maintained with China and with Turkey.
The most important figure in the literary and artistic
world of the period was Sultān Husayn ibn Bayqara of
Herat. Even politically he is not to be despised, and he
alone of the descendants of Tīmūr managed to maintain
his throne for thirty-eight years till his death in 1506.
This was largely due to the wisdom and justice of his
minister, Mīr 'Ali Shīr, who had played with him in
childhood and who was, like his master, a poet as well
as a patron. Apart from being a most attractive figure

53

on account of his faithfulness and modesty, Mīr 'Alī Shīr probably did more for Persian painting than any other man. He is the real founder of the great school of Herat. There is no need to lay too much emphasis on the place: it is probably fanciful to look for a rockier, more barren landscape in the miniatures executed there than in the more fertile neighbourhood of Shirāz. But as a state capital for so long where beautiful books were so much appreciated and were the most valued presents from one prince to another, Herat naturally attracted all the best artists. The establishment of a school there meant a quite definite system of pupilage as among the calligraphers: thus Bihzād was the pupil of Pīr Sayyid Ahmad of Tabrīz. The artist's position was at last more adequately recognised; but this stability for the artist was accompanied by a stability, almost a crystallisation, of the art-form. Any divergence within the standard form is a personal matter: so that attribution, and not dating, is now the important question. The fifteenth century, or more exactly the period from 1440 to 1520, is homogeneous. If one can trace the rise of certain artists to the height of their power it is as much as can be expected. It cannot be too much emphasised that the Persians are a very conservative people.

That there was no new development in the classical school at Herat is evident from a comparison of some of its products with some of the earlier fifteenth-century manuscripts made there or elsewhere. The Gulbenkian manuscript has already been mentioned as containing some miniatures that belong to this fully developed Timurid style. Even closer parallels will be found in another manuscript of 1410, the Iskandernāma in the British Museum, several miniatures of which are remarkably similar to those in the Nizāmī attributed to Bihzād. Apart from these there is no doubt that many manuscripts must have been produced by the body of forty calligraphers and artists assembled by Shāh Rukh's son Baysunqur (1396–1433) under Mawlānā Jaʿfar of Tabrīz. He was governor of Astarabad, but Schulz suggests that his artists were drawn from Baghdad and Tabrīz. Certainly the Timurids were responsible for extending the Persian school eastwards.

A very fine copy of the Shāh-nāma which appears to have been executed for Mohammed Jūkī (d. 1444), a brother of Baysunqur, is in the possession of the Royal Asiatic Society. It is an excellent example of the mid-Timurid period, and shows to great advantage the state of miniature painting the generation before Bihzād appeared on the scene. There is nothing lacking from these miniatures in richness of colouring or exquisite minuteness of detail. The coral-like mountains are of every colour, blue, violet, maroon and orange: a great deal of gold is used and a particularly marvellous green which has lasted wonderfully well. Plate 5 shows some of these qualities and also the eye for dramatic effect that the artist had. Farūd has just shot the arrow that pins Zarāsp to the saddle: his hand is still raised as he watches its flight. Zarāsp is reeling in the saddle, his horse bends the other way. Tūs and his army are ranged in the right-hand corner and along the foreground. In the background is the mountain fastness of Mount Sapad, with a Cufic inscription over the gate. The artist has also introduced bare branches which were effectively used at this period.[1] One of the most marvellous miniatures in this manuscript represents a cavalry battle on a green slope in quite amazing detail: unfortunately it is too minute in style to reproduce well. Elephants are represented in several of them, and in one is a very rare subject, the simurgh (looking like a phœnix) rescuing the baby child of Sām from exposure on a rock. After

[1] For the story illustrated see A. G. Warner and E. Warner, " The Shahnama," Vol. III. pp. 37–109, and particularly p. 53.

5. Farūd slays Zarāsp on Mount Sapad.

seeing this manuscript one must admit that Bihzād had precursors who were great artists but whose names probably do not survive.

But it is time to consider the great master himself whose fame was so great that it has eclipsed that of predecessors, contemporaries and successors alike. It is impossible to avoid being controversial when talking of his work. As has been said before, the main problem of the later fifteenth century is one of attribution. So far it has not been advanced very far. All the manuscripts which might provide a firm basis for the study of Bihzād's art are suspected by some authority. One of the main difficulties is that the names attached to these miniatures are attributions and not autograph signatures. Even those concealed in minute script between the margins or on the field of the miniatures are not beyond suspicion. There are two alternative explanations for these signatures if they are not genuine contemporary ascriptions by the calligrapher: they may either represent later, often much later, attributions, or the miniatures with their artists' names may have been copied by later painters in Persia or even in India. Both suspicions have been cast at the manuscript in the British Museum (Or. 6810) which is dated 1494–5, and which contains signatures of Bihzād, Mīrak and Qāsim 'Alī. There are certainly two and possibly three hands to be traced in this famous manuscript. One is more markedly academic and may very well be that of Mīrak: his identity will be discussed later. The more lively miniatures have long been attributed to Bihzād in virtue of the ascriptions beneath, in what Sir Thomas Arnold describes as " a good old perhaps contemporary calligraphy." Many of these miniatures also bear signatures of Qāsim 'Alī, several concealed in the miniatures. This has led the French critics to attribute all these remaining miniatures to the hand of one who is only once mentioned in the literary sources which now begin to take small notice of painters, and then as a portraitist. Closer examination of the manuscript reveals an inequality of technique among these miniatures, though the compositions are all most vigorous and fresh. This fact has led Dr. Martin and Sir Thomas Arnold to attribute eight of these to the hand of Bihzād himself, while supposing that the remainder were finished by Qāsim 'Alī after Bihzād's sketches. Though it is not strictly the case that " the attributions to Bihzād are written on all those miniatures which have not got the signature of Qāsim 'Alī," some such division of work between the master and his school seems highly probable. The scene reproduced on Plate 7 must preserve at least a composition from his hand. It is full of life and shows his favourite blue predominating as the colour of the bathing drawers: the towels evidently provided the artist with an opportunity for experimenting with pattern. One is struck by the naturalness of the gestures of the men engaged in this typical Oriental scene.

This is mature work: Bihzād was probably born about 1450. An example of his earlier work, also in the British Museum, which really seems above suspicion, is a manuscript of Nizāmī written in 1442 (Add. 25,900). Three of the miniatures in it have a signature of Bihzād interpolated between the column margins of the text in the corner of the painting. The writing seems to be that of the calligrapher of the text, who has thus filled in this extract of the poem after the miniature was drawn. But more convincing is the style of the work itself. There are two other hands visible in this manuscript and some of the pages are still left blank. One is much later, rather stiff and gaudy, and, as is shown by the bâtons in the turbans, of Safavid date. These are the last miniatures in the volume. The other appears to be contemporary with Bihzād, and his work is scattered through

the earlier part.   Possibly even one or two more are by
Bihzād, and they are all close enough to be studio work.
The palette is much the same as in the signed paintings—
pale turquoise, a pale green and an olive, yellow, vermilion
and crimson with gold and silver; but the colours are
not used with such restraint or discretion and the drawing,
though minute, has not the amazing firmness and vir-
tuosity of Bihzād's own work.   In technical excellence
these drawings by Bihzād are equal to those in the
Royal Asiatic Society Shāh-nāma: the composition is
not more advanced, but there is a greater interest in
personality.   In his picture of the battle between the
clans of Layla and Majnūn the camels gnash their teeth
and their eyes shine fiercely, the iris picked out with
gold.   He reserves a good proportion of the field as a
neutral passage, and his tone is much cooler than is
usual in Persian miniature painting.   The vermilion and
gold are used sparingly but with great effect.

Of course these must have been executed many years
after 1442 (when Bihzād was probably not born), but
the close similarity with work of the previous generation
would point to an early period in his career, before he
had begun to develop great individuality, say about
1475.   This would bring it close in date to a manuscript

6. A DISPUTATION OF DOCTORS.

of the Būstān of Sā'dī belonging to Mr. Chester Beatty which is attributed to Bihzād, and which is, in fact, very similar in style. It has the same blues, cool-coloured rocks, and gold eyes, and the same easy grace of attitude. It is quite possible that all its eleven miniatures are by him. But another copy of the same poem in the Khedival Library at Cairo and dated 1488 seems to be by quite another hand.

Midway between the two manuscripts at the British Museum would come another in Mr. Chester Beatty's collection which is dated 1485, and contains thirteen miniatures which are given to Bihzād in the colophon of the manuscript. But though this ascription appears to be written in the hand of the calligrapher it would be unwise to accept it too definitely. In character this copy of Mīr Khusrau Dihlavi's Khamsa is different from either and rather closer to the Cairo Sa'dī. In the rather violent gestures and the taller figures it may perhaps be associated with other dervish scenes in a manuscript in the Cartier collection published by M. Sakisian as the work of Sultān Mohammed. These represent another more academic school of which a good many manuscripts from just round this date have survived. From the same year, 1485, comes a copy of Mīr

5

'Alī Shīr's " String Of Jewels " in the Bodleian Library. This poem had only been written two years before this date by the minister of Sultān Bayqara who was Bihzād's first patron. He was himself an illuminator, he had a fine library, and he showed the anxiety to retire from the world which is the main outward sign of Sufiism. He did indeed join a dervish order, that of Naqshbandiyya. The great body of miniature painters at Herat seem to have worked especially for patrons affected by this mystical philosophy of contemplation which was the natural resource for thinking men in a country disturbed by constant wars and with a foreign army camped in its midst. The artists of scenes like that on Plate 6 sought almost too desperately to fill their miniatures with scenes that would not only charm the eye but also divert the mind. They filled them with carpets and tiles and calligraphic architecture: trees and rocks with gazelles upon them, and above all the plane tree with its variegated leaves and gleaming silvery trunk. These are not illustrations but invitations to absorption in nature: they have an inner meaning like the odes of Hafiz, but the artists are perhaps equally ready to forget it.

Such a reflection is necessary to show by contrast the more conservative character of Bihzād, who was no Sufi but the last and greatest exponent of the illustrative style. The more peaceful miniatures in the British Museum, Nizāmī of 1494 and of 1442, are those which must be attributed to other hands. Two school scenes in particular and one of Sikandar disputing with the doctors are among those not by him. On the contrary, Bihzād seems happiest in battle scenes: all three of the signed miniatures represent combats. One is a battle scene on a minute scale like those in the R.A.S. manuscript, one of the traditional combat of the clans of Layla and Majnūn, and the third of Bihram Gur slaying the dragon. This is an additional reason for ascribing to Bihzād the miniatures in the Zafar-nāma, now in the possession of Mr. Garrett and published in colour by Sir Thomas Arnold. It was copied in 1467 for the library of Sultān Husayn and afterwards passed into that of the Mughal emperors. There is no signature of Bihzād, but the Emperor Jahāngīr, when he inherited the manuscript, recorded in a note in it the opinion of his father Akbar that it was from the master's hand. He may have carried out his work in it at any time previous to 1505, when Sultān Husayn died: from the developed style it is probably rather near this date, and there had been time for the manuscript to get so thumbed as to be remarginated first. The miniatures, which illustrate the campaigns of Tīmūr, are naturally warlike and full of movement. The figures are not on so minute a scale as in the Nizāmī, though the colouring is very similar. The twelve miniatures are in pairs on double pages which together form one composition. An example of this device for enlarging the field is to be seen on Plate 11.

Full use is made by Bihzād of the traditional means of arranging a large number of figures on different planes by placing them among mountains and on towers, but he seems to have realised that such effects were lacking in unity, and he has in some of these miniatures introduced ropes which, being white, stand out sharply and pull the composition together. This device was afterwards extensively copied, as, for instance, in the Nizāmī of Shāh Tahmāsp, and in a page recently acquired by the Victoria and Albert Museum.

Another manuscript at St. Petersburg was given by Schulz and Dr. Martin to Bihzād and the period after 1500. But there is certainly a great lack of material for this period. The traditional date of his death is 1534, although Sir T. Arnold thinks he may have died about ten years earlier. But it is known that, after the fall of his old patron, Sultān Husayn, in 1505, Bihzād moved

7. Scene in a Public Bath. *By Bihzād.*

to the court of the new Safavid prince Ismā'īl at Tabrīz in north-west Persia. A document dated 1522 survives in which Shāh Ismā'īl appointed Bihzād head of all his library staff, calligraphers, gilders, painters and marginators. Complete obedience to him is enjoined and there is a notable coupling of painting and calligraphy as equally divine gifts.

It is possible that Bihzād was henceforth so much engaged in superintending this large establishment that he had not much time to work himself: but, of course, many other works must have been executed by him, and some others may still survive. It has been customary to fill the gap with the large number of detached miniatures which bear signatures of Bihzād or which are similar in style to those that do. This second glory of Persian painting begins at about this date, the earliest examples being finished portraits with carefully drawn heads and brightly tinted robes. One of the best known types of these which must be mentioned is the portrait of a prisoner of high rank with his neck and arm in a yoke or palahang. The original of this must have been a very fine thing, and with their conservative feeling, the artists went on producing versions of it for fifty years. Another well-known subject is that of the youthful Shāh

Tahmāsp who succeeded to the throne in 1524 at the age of thirteen. Bihzād may have treated both of these subjects, but it is difficult to say if an original by him is actually in existence. Certainly it is not easy to think of him as the originator of a new style: he was the perfect craftsman: if the portrait of him, published by M. Sakisian, is to be believed, a small studious man who must have won the admiration of his contemporaries and his patrons by the extraordinary steadiness of his line; who welcomed the opportunity of portraying emotion to show skill rather than to make a portrait, and whose innovations were in detail and arrangement and not in conception. Remembering this it is not easy to trace the influence of Bihzād on Persian painting. The names of his pupils are preserved and work signed by several of them has survived; but there is very little sign of a true school of painting in the Western sense. No doubt what could be passed on was just that normal Persian regard for the qualities of his craft, colour and line, raised to the highest power. In fact he had brought self-consciousness almost to excess and ousted the semi-legendary Mānī from his position of father of the art of painting, substituting a human ideal of excellence.

CHAPTER VI

THE SAFAVIDS

S o long ago as 1912 Mr. Clive Bell was pointing out the mistake of regarding Bihzād as the earliest great master of Persia. It seems now more necessary to put in a plea for the succeeding age, which cannot in any sense be considered a period of artistic decadence. The reputation of Bihzād was in some ways a misfortune for the art, but there is certainly no lack of invention among his successors. Fortunately, too, there is a great bulk of manuscripts and miniatures surviving from this period, so that its characteristics can be more easily and more fully grasped. The intolerance towards painters had now practically ceased; and though they themselves were still humble craftsmen, their work was in greater request, and such patrons as Shāh Tahmāsp were insatiable in their demands. There is consequently a good deal of painting by the yard, as in a famous manuscript of the Shāh-nāma belonging to Baron Eduard de Rothschild, for which he insisted on 276 miniatures, which, though it

is always charmingly decorative, is apt to appear somewhat monotonous.   But there are plenty of masterpieces
besides and a bewildering number of names in the literary
sources and at the foot of miniatures.   Unfortunately
most of these names are so common as to be insufficient
material for identification.

The general character of the period is extremely
conservative: a satisfactory palette and style have been
found, and the artists are wise enough not to experiment
much in technique.   They devote all their attention to
composition and subject-matter.   The biggest demand is
evidently for the old classics of Persian literature, the works
of Nizāmī, Firdausī and Sāʿdī and more rarely for Ḥafiz.
The Safavid dynasty which mounted the throne in 1502
strengthened its claim with a descent, whether true or
fabricated, from the ancient Pehlevi kings of Persia and
with nationalist aims.   A certain archaism is therefore
to be expected in the art of the period, but this is not much
more marked than in most periods of Persian history.
There is no need to think of this old-fashioned work being
produced only at distant centres like Bukhara.   Painting
in Persia had always been Persian, so that the main change
is the appearance of the bâton round which the turbans
of the followers of this house were wound.   This family

8. Majnūn watches the Battle of the Clans.

distinction, which became the crest of the whole country, when its position was established, should properly be red and is always so represented in miniatures at first; but later, when it ceased to be of such importance, after all opposition disappeared, the artist and possibly the wearer took liberties with its colour, choosing one which toned with his costume—blue or black. After the death of Shāh Tahmāsp in 1574 it seems to have almost disappeared.

The miniature reproduced on Plate 8 from a manuscript of Nizāmī dated 1500, and presumably illuminated a year or two later, shows the archaising tendency right at the beginning of this period. The artist in depicting the well-worn subject of the battle between the clans of Layla and Majnūn, which is watched in desolation by the horror-struck Majnūn, on whose account they are fighting, has borrowed some of Bihzād's liveliness but is evidently unable to treat the scene *au grand sérieux*. The mad anguish of Majnūn is rather well shown, but the miniaturist was more interested in the pattern of his camels than in the fight. It is a typical piece of work.

Very different in quality is another copy of Nizāmī's five poems which was executed for Shāh Tahmāsp himself by the royal artists at Tabrīz, between 1539 and 1543.

It is now in the British Museum and colour-plates of its fourteen contemporary miniatures have been published by Mr. Binyon in a monograph, so that they are easily accessible. In addition, each of the three hundred and ninety-six leaves is surrounded with decorative painting in gold, of beasts, natural and supernatural, among running foliage. The beauty is enhanced by varying the thickness of the gold so that it appears now greener, now yellower. Most of the miniatures are signed with the artists' names: though it seems that they did not themselves write these signatures, they are almost certainly contemporary and reliable. Though five artists seemed to have worked at the volume, the style is very similar in all these miniatures. This manuscript is certainly one of the most marvellous examples of Persian art; it is more impressive than any surviving work of Bihzād to the writer's eye at least, which is better able to appreciate the big compositions than the minute work of Bihzād. There is fine detail in this manuscript, too, as can be seen from Plate 9, but the treatment is certainly broader.

This charming arcadian scene is introduced by Mīr Sayyid 'Alī into a picture illustrating the story of Layla and Majnūn. It is very typical of the purposely dis-

9. Pastoral Scene (detail).   *By Mīr Sayyid ʿAlī.*

cursive work of these artists. They seem also to have
responded to a demand for pictures of country life.
Persians are naturally a town-loving people, but they
like to go out into the country to picnic and talk. It is
natural in this way to see the country as a paradise, but
such scenes of agriculture were not only peaceful to the
mind of the onlooker, they were also reminders of the
return of peace with the Safavid dynasty to the much-
harassed countryside. There are a number of tinted
sketches of ploughing and milking which belonged to
about the middle of the sixteenth century and which are
conjecturally associated with the name Mohammadi.
Of Mīr Sayyid 'Alī's own work not much survives, but he
is of great importance because, with 'Abd-us-Samad of
Shirāz, he accompanied Humāyūn to Kabul in 1550 and
was head of the school which developed the Mughal
style. He was a poet as well, so that it is not surprising
that he had not much time to devote to painting. But
it is possible that he alone, or the two Court painters
together, painted for Humāyūn when he was in exile at
Tabrīz, as a kind of diploma picture, a portrait-group of
the whole house of Tīmūr, which was afterwards taken to
India and added to there. After unknown vicissitudes,
and having suffered terribly, it is now in the British

Museum. The scarcity of paper would account for this large painting having been executed on linen; and in its present damaged state it is not easy to judge of it. But in spite of brilliance of colouring it is not altogether a satisfactory work. It is too diffuse, the gigantic plane tree in the middle not quite holding the whole together. It seems that the Persians were not really capable of dealing with an area more than a foot either way. A similar " durbar " composition in miniature, which was exhibited at Paris in 1912, seems far more satisfactory. As an historical document, of course, the painting is of the very greatest importance.

Of the other painters who illustrated Shāh Tahmāsp's Nizāmī, the most prominent is Mīrak, to whom five of the miniatures are assigned. It is questionable on grounds of style if this can be the same artist as the Mīrak who collaborated with Bihzād and Qāsim 'Alī in the Nizāmī of 1494. The problem is typical of the difficulty of attributing Persian miniatures, especially when they are signed. As long ago as 1908 M. Huart assumed the existence of two painters of the name and of a calligrapher who decorated the mosques of Herat. But, in any case, the more prominent artist who is stated by Iskandar Munshī, who wrote in 1629, to have been a personal friend of Shāh

Tahmāsp and his boon companion at drinking bouts, must have been the illustrator of this book. The earlier artist of the 1494 Nizāmī with his somewhat dry academic style is probably the man who is mentioned by Khwanda-mīr (1524) as having accompanied Bābur to Kabul in 1507–8, and having died soon afterwards before 1510. But the name is a common one. According to Sir Thomas Arnold this is the calligrapher.

Three of the miniatures in this Nizāmī of 1539 are scenes from the romantic love story of Khusrau and Shīrīn and are laid at Khusrau's court, crowded with figures in the most gorgeous costumes. All the fashions of the period for both men and women can be studied. Probably at no period have such beautiful materials, such excellent pure colours and such lovely designs been worn. The general shape of Persian clothes except the turbans remained unchanged for centuries, but previously the materials, except perhaps for the collar, had been plain. Now, not only are they covered with dot and flower patterns, but also a repeat pattern in clouds or birds, something after the style of the gold borders of this manuscript, and rather reminiscent of Chinese taste, were introduced. It is probably at about this period, in the first half of the sixteenth century, that many of the

drawings of Chinese design, of which there are several at
Constantinople, in the old Imperial collection, were made.
Examples are reproduced by Kühnel and Sakisian.
There was as great a rage for *chinoiserie* as in the eighteenth
century in England. Similar dresses may be seen in the
double frontispiece to a copy of the story of Yūsuf and
Zulaykhā by Jāmī, which is dated 1569 (Plate 11).
Fashions had, by then, become even more extreme:
hares are to be seen to the left, and on one pair of trousers,
easily visible beneath the tucked-up skirts, is a strange
pattern in pale blue which looks like " eyes." The
composition is very effective with its dark foreground,
ending abruptly in a light range of hills.

Many sketches of single figures thus exquisitely dressed
belong to this period or a little earlier. Most of these
exquisites are young men, and among them are several
supposed portraits of Tahmāsp himself, who came to the
throne in 1524. When Dr. Martin wrote in 1912, he gave
this whole class to Sultān Mohammed, who is the last
important illustrator of Tahmāsp's big Nizāmī. His
paintings are spacious and very charming, and he was
evidently a good painter of animals: of horses in particular, which show more than the usual distinction of the
Persian miniature school. The figures are graceful and

10. PICNIC PARTY (UNFINISHED). *School of Muhammadī.*

lively, but there is nothing to make one believe that he
was a great portrait painter. Consequently, there is
reason to admit M. Sakisian's division of Dr. Martin's
Sultān Mohammed into several personalities, of whom
one was named Mohammed Mumin and another Shaikh
Mohammed. English collections are rather weak in the
style of detached miniatures, in which the Paris collections are so rich. One of the most famous, that of M.
Goloubew, is now in the Museum of Fine Arts at Boston.
But there is a charming picture of a young man in gold
brocade with a narcissus in his turban in the British
Museum, with an inscription, perhaps false, stating that
it is a copy by Rizā after Sultān Mohammed.

By the end of the reign of Shāh Tahmāsp in 1574,
artists under the lead of their aristocratic patrons had
become further emancipated from their old illustrative
work. Even such miniatures as that reproduced on
Plate 11 have very little to do with the poem which
follows. More and more the best artists would be
occupied in doing portrait sketches and such sketches as
that of the Picnic, reproduced on Plate 10. This is called
unfinished, and it certainly gives a most interesting idea of
the miniature artist's technique, but it is quite likely that
this curious effect of carefully finished faces and hands

and sketched outline was intentional. It is a *tour de force* intended for the album of some connoisseur. There is a negro introduced into the composition, without which, it has been exaggeratedly said, Bihzād never painted a miniature in order to show to advantage the clear complexion of the other figures. It has been attributed to Mohammadi, who certainly did lightly tinted sketches, as mentioned above, and whose signature is also to be found attached to some *fantaisie* sketches of loving couples. But there is really no particular reason to connect it with him.

Now that the painter is emancipated from his extremely subordinate relation to the calligrapher, his art has gained in dignity, and has now itself won a position of influence over textile designs. Such patterns as that on a Persian brocade at South Kensington (Plate 12) are clearly borrowed from miniature painting. A fine collection of such stuffs still survives at the Castle of Rosenborg near Copenhagen, to which they were brought back by ambassadors in the early seventeenth century. The piece reproduced, with its endless repetition backwards and forwards of the same sad scene of Layla and Majnūn, was yet gaily worn by some Persian, quite oblivious of the pathos of this meeting in the desert between the two

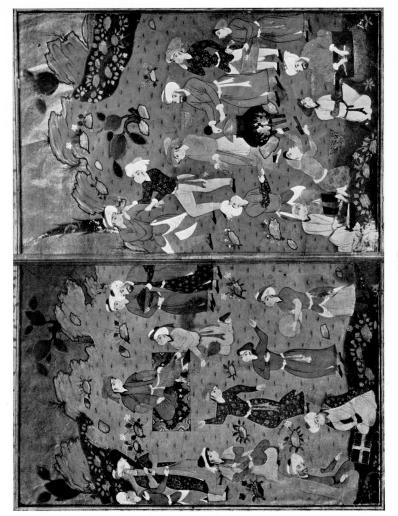

11. A Picnic.

lovers, achieved after many struggles, but when Majnūn's reason was indeed so far weakened as to be unable to bear or perhaps appreciate the joy they might have had. Of course, everyone was familiar with the story: in wearing this stuff he would merely be identifying himself with the heroic age, so much pleasanter than the actual present.

6

CHAPTER VII

THE LAST PHASE: EUROPEAN INFLUENCE

I n later Safavid times the artist's work is very much more varied: as European influence increased, he was completely emancipated from the book, and in the eighteenth century finally produced full-length portraits to be hung in public rooms. Schulz reproduces some frescoes in the Palace of Eriwan: in many of the fifteenth-century miniatures are smaller wall paintings, usually done in blue outline on a white ground. Some of these are purely formal with conventionalised flowers, but several contain figures. These are usually represented in bedroom scenes, and if these are not purely imaginary fantasies on the part of the artist, must have been confined to the woman's quarters. In rather a different class are those illustrating the story of Joseph and Zulaykha, in which one incident is the attempt by Zulaykha to win Joseph's love by forcing him to look at her. She took him into a Pavilion which she had had painted with a number of pictures on walls, floor and ceiling of Joseph

78

and herself in affectionate attitudes. Joseph was on the point of giving way when he noticed a curtain in the corner which, being pulled aside, revealed her god which Zulaykha had thus tried to prevent from witnessing the scene. Sir Thomas Arnold has published a miniature of this scene from a manuscript in the Bodleian Library (" Painting in Islam," Plate 32). The incidents are artificially arranged in a sort of gilt iconostasis.

In another manuscript of this poem of Yūsuf and Zulaykha, dated 1569, and also in the Bodleian, the artist has carried to an extreme length certain tendencies which have been insisted on throughout the history of Persian painting. The miniature reproduced as Plate 13 can be paralleled by several others in this manuscript. It represents Zulaykha coming into the garden where she has left the maidens, so that one among them may win Joseph's love, which she intended to profit by herself. The foreground is paved, and the paving ends abruptly at the foot of a steep hill, which is coloured pink, and completely covered with a formalised whirl design. Behind this rises another hill, which has a number of small plants growing over it, geometrically disposed. The outline against the sky is very thickly drawn, and is rather like that in the early manuscript belonging to the

Royal Asiatic Society. It is, perhaps, a misunderstood convention for indicating shrubs seen against the sky-line. The carpet appears to stand stiffly upright between pavement and hill. The figures are grouped in the most artificial way, the artist preserving the simplest form of balance. The Persian love of decorative design and balanced confrontation has triumphed here completely over naturalism. Only the figure of Joseph himself with his beautiful pear-shaped, flaming gold halo has much natural grace. The colouring, improbable though it is, makes of the whole a charming scene, and such simplification is certainly preferable to some of the over-elaborated compositions like some large paintings at the Hermitage from this period.

But most artists of this later period preferred the quicker style of the pen drawing, usually faintly tinted, to the more elaborate and longer task of illuminating manuscripts. The art became more popular because it was more easily accessible: these drawings cost very little to produce. The best of them are associated with the name of Rizā, about which a great controversy, mostly in German, raged just before the war. It is not necessary to go here into all the evidence produced by Karabacek, Sarre and Mittwoch, Blochet and Sakisian,

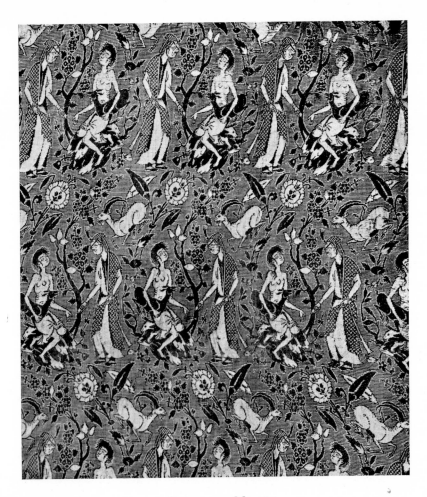

12. Layla and Majnūn.

but it does seem probable, though Sir Thomas Arnold never agreed, that there were at least two major artists of the name, the first of whom may conveniently be known as Aqā Rizā; for Aqā means the older; and the second as Rizā-ī-'Abbāsi, for he first worked, at any rate, under Shāh 'Abbās the Great (1587–1629). These are only two of several different variants of signatures and descriptions appended to these drawings. For Aqā Rizā there is a reference in the work of Iskandar Munshī published in 1629, where he is described as dissolute in his habits, but a friend of Shāh 'Abbās. He was, presumably, then in his old age, if he was a pupil of Mīr 'Ali of Herat (died 1544). He may, perhaps, have died about 1595. Although it is probable that he never signed himself Aqā Rizā, these names are convenient for grouping two different styles. The first is a linear school, developing the earlier sixteenth-century pen drawing into a most vigorous, sometimes almost impressionistic art. Though the portrait of a doctor, formerly absurdly said to be Avicenna (Frontispiece), has not the same vigour as some of these drawings where the pen has sometimes even spluttered at the end of a stroke, the line is extremely beautiful; the long full curve of the back being formed of three separate segments perfectly con-

nected. The drawing of the beard is a very beautiful
and typical example of this work at its most fastidious:
the buttons and sleeves are slightly touched with gold.
In calling it " school of Aqā Rizā " there is simply a
desire to associate it with this style and a date about 1590.

For the most part the safest way of dating these drawings produced between 1550 and 1650 is by the head-
dress. At the end of the reign of Shāh Tahmāsp the
turban, which had been gradually growing larger and
more elaborate, suddenly grew to an immense size, so
unwieldly that it was soon varied with a number of other
types of head-covering, especially a soft hat with a fur
border, and a curious affair rather like a cocked hat.
Under Shāh 'Abbās too, for the first time, the long-
waisted robe gives way to a short flounced jacket, often
also edged with fur, while for women the head-dress, the
ends of which had been hanging right down the back,
became suddenly joined with the cloak in a sort of hood.
Costumes of this type are represented in the little Elzevir
duodecimo on Persia published in 1633, though it is not
clear who was responsible for these woodcuts. Finally,
under Shāh 'Abbās II (1642–67) the dress materials,
which had been increasingly rich, became again much
plainer and heavier, depending for relief on trimmings.

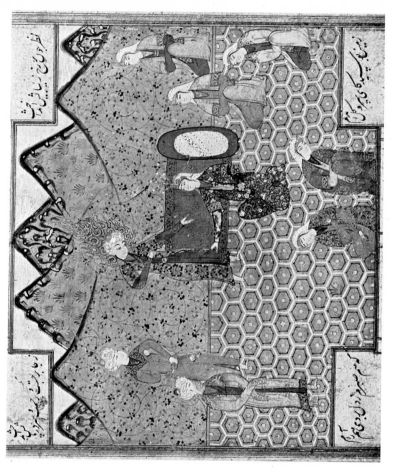

13. Joseph resisting the Graces of Zulaykhá.

During the seventeenth century European influence, which had been at work for quite a hundred years, became rather more noticeable; but it never became predominant. The Persians with their great inquisitiveness and avid interest in the habits of foreigners, noticed so amusingly by Sir John Malcolm in his " Sketches in Persia," were naturally very much interested in European art. And it certainly enjoyed a limited vogue; but, except for a few details, it was not assimilated into the art of the country. From so early as the first half of the sixteenth century comes an album in the Bibliothèque Nationale (Pers. 129) in which are inserted some engravings by Dürer. No doubt as early as this they began copying such engravings, most of which must have reached the country through the missionaries established there. It is worth noticing that there was a College of Oriental Languages established at Isfahan by the Discalced Carmelites. The great majority of these engravings were consequently religious and provided a new iconography, as well as a new style, for the copyist. He sometimes copied as accurately as possible, though naturally in a colouring that would have astonished the original artist. But more often the central part of the design only would be copied and native figures or landscape introduced round about. Beyond these come all sorts of stages down to sheer parody. There is literary evidence that under Shāh Ismāʿil (1502–24), Mawlānā Mohammed Sabzavari, a highly skilled copyist of calligraphy, studied European painting. Iskandar Munshī says that he excelled at this kind of work. Later on, in the second half of the seventeenth century, a Persian artist even went to Rome to study painting: on his return he added two miniatures to the big Nizāmī of Shāh Tahmāsp in the British Museum. One of these is reproduced in colour by Sir Thomas Arnold, who gives the evidence for his life. They are rather surprisingly Persian in style.

Although pictures in the European style are by no means rare, only a few details were adopted from them by the Persian artist in his ordinary work. The greatest name in the seventeenth century is that of Rizā-i-ʿAbbāsi. M. Sakisian gives the extreme dates of his activity, taken from dated miniatures, as 1618 to 1639. He seems unjustified in saying that he could not, therefore, have received his surname from Shāh ʿAbbās, who died in 1629: surely there is time enough during the eleven years between 1618 and 1629. And in any case M. Blochet [1] publishes miniatures dated 1613 and 1615. This does

[1] " Les Enluminures," p. 150.

not give a very long *floruit*, and it must be further extended :
in the British Museum is a large illuminated page from a
manuscript which is signed and dated 1640 on the field
of the miniature. And in this late example the only
distinct trace of European influence is in the clouds,
which, instead of being rendered in the Chinese " tai "
convention, are not very successfully indicated with
wisps of Chinese white.

There is a manuscript in the Victoria and Albert
Museum of Nizāmī's " Khusrau and Shīrīn " with seven-
teen miniatures, all signed by Rizā-i-'Abbāsi. One of
them has been chosen for reproduction here (Plate 15)
because, although, as has been explained, these manuscript illustrations are no longer the typical product, it
shows by comparison with an earlier treatment of the
story, as, for instance, in the Nizāmī of 1539, how greatly
the point of view has changed. One of the miniatures
is dated 1632, and this must be taken as the real date of
them all, in spite of the fact that the colophon of the
manuscript contains the date, unmistakably spelt out in
full, 1680. Sir Thomas Arnold, who published this
manuscript,[1] suggested that the calligrapher must have
worked with such care as to take forty-eight years over

[1] In the *Burlington Magazine*, January 1921.

the work. This does not seem possible; and, besides, the calligrapher Abdul Jabbār of Isfahan seems to have died in 1655. He copied a manuscript now in the Bibliothèque Nationale in 1620–24. Of course it is possible that both the painter and the calligrapher, Riza i-'Abbāsi and Abdul Jabbār, are each of them " different men of the same name ": but the style of painting and the fashion of the clothes do correspond exactly to 1632. The date in the colophon must remain one of those many insoluble puzzles with which the study of Persian painting is unfortunately darkened.

By 1632 then, the figures in these miniatures are no longer at all heroic: Farhād falling in love with Shirīn at first sight, is a very ordinary man with long moustaches: she is a coquette with a flower. All the people are vulgar figures from the bazaar. Their clothes too are not elaborate, and the vegetation is indicated in light gold outline which seems to have strayed from the border into the field of the miniature. The artist has not troubled to produce a very finished effect. The whole is still certainly decorative and Riza is an artist who was ready to experiment. The mixed colours in these miniatures may not be very satisfactory, but they are interesting. The commonest colours are purple, indigo and yellow;

14. LADY RECLINING. *By Mir Afzal of Tūn.*

and the heavy folds in the robes are indicated with similar colours in a much deeper tone. This may be the result of observation, but it is much exaggerated.

Probably a prominent artist like Rizā was less influenced by the democratic taste of the day than most. But he has shown his low ideal in these paintings, and his more normal work usually depicts tipsy pages, though he was not averse from drawing old men. Some of these page-boys have a kind of stippled pink complexion which must certainly be derived from some European original. In these later miniatures it is evident how much Persian painting lacked a tradition among its public; but this was made good to an amazing degree by the natural taste of the artist. It was responsible for the sensuousness of these drawings, but they never cease to be charmingly rendered.

Nothing could be more typical of this than the minia-ture reproduced on Plate 14. There is nothing known of the artist, who has signed himself Mīr Afzal of Tūn, unless he is the same man who signs plain Afzal on a miniature published by Schulz from St. Petersburg. This is not likely, because Mīr (which also means " prince ") must in this case be an inseparable part of his name. This languid lady reclines on three cushions, one gold, one blue and one brown. They rest on nothing in particular. She wears a blue robe lined with green, and her trousers are white above with blue and gold design, and very decorated blue below on the part more normally visible. She has bare feet and her hair hangs in very long plaits. In the foreground are some accessories that increase the languorous impression: an absurd pet dog with a glowing gold eye, for which Bihzād must be held responsible, drinks from a Chinese bowl; another blue-and-white pot on the other side holds roses. On both the original Ming design has been " improved " by the addition of native elements by the artist, amongst which a mosque with minarets is visible. The background is simply a faintly indicated gold palm. She is certainly charming, but there is no mistaking her vulgarity.

This school is the last at all worthy of Persia until this century, when there has been an attempt to revive the older style. Afterwards there was nothing but slavish copying of the old illuminated manuscripts by hacks, and later some academic portraits in the European style. The only new production in the nineteenth century was a series of portraits and decorative panels for hammams in a flat " signboard " technique, not unamusing with

15. MEETING OF FARHAD AND SHÍRÍN. *By Riẓā 'Abbāsī.*

their very bright colours. The faces, with an attempt at modelling in the European style, show the same exaggeration of features and mixture of frontal and side view which is typical of the Roman sarcophagus portraits from the fayūm. Occasional examples of landscape in this style may be seen: at their best they are superficially reminiscent of the *douanier* Rousseau. These are pictures on canvas or panel and painted with European colours.

Europe, in fact, has done very little for Persian art: the balance is heavily against her. Leaving aside any question of the ultimate origin of miniature painting, both Flemish and Italian artists showed their appreciation of Persian art. Carpets and faience occur frequently, especially in the pictures of the Venetian school. The study of their styles is likely to throw light on the chronology of both the original and the painting. The greatest direct contribution of the Persian book has been from the binding: Eastern bindings were exactly copied in Venice in the fifteenth and sixteenth centuries, and these designs were carried all over Europe. Many of the standard binders' ornaments are of Persian origin. But perhaps bookbinding might do well to return for fresh inspiration to the original source.

More directly connected with miniature painting and

the greatest contribution of Persian art to Europe [1] are the designs, particularly the figure designs, which have been constantly repeated on Western looms down to the present, and which, as was previously explained, originally derive from miniatures. A number of these are to be found in leading furnishers' in London to-day, though not always with due honour given to their origin. But, once more, the designing trade might profitably turn to the prototypes of these designs in the miniatures, and extract new motives from them. The border designs in freehand and stencilling provide ideas that are almost ready to be used.

[1] Note also the Persian influence in the South Russian school of Ikon-painting.

BIBLIOGRAPHY

I. The following large books contain a rich series of reproductions of miniatures :

F. R. Martin : The Miniature Painting and Painters of Persia, India and Turkey from the eighth to the eighteenth century. 2 vols. *London,* 1912. 4°.

W. P. Schulz : Die persisch-islamische Miniaturmalerei. 2 vols. *Leipzig,* 1914. 4°.

G. Marteau and H. Vever : Miniatures persanes . . . exposées au Musée des Arts décoratifs, juin–octobre 1912. 2 vols. *Paris,* 1913. Fol.

E. Blochet : Les Peintures des manuscrits orientaux de la Bibliothèque Nationale. *Paris,* 1920. 4°.

E. Blochet : Les Enluminures des manuscrits orientaux de la Bibliothèque Nationale. *Paris,* 1926. 4°.

A. M. Coomaraswamy : Les Miniatures orientales de la collection Goloubew au Museum of Fine Arts de Boston. *Paris ; Bruxelles,* 1929. 4°.

A. Sakisian : La Miniature persane du XIIe au XVIIe siècle. *Paris ; Bruxelles,* 1929. 4°.

E. Blochet : Musulman Painting XIIth–XVIIth-century. Translated by Cicely M. Binyon. *London,* 1929. 8°.

A useful selection is contained in :

E. Kühnel : Miniaturmalerei im islamischen Orient. *Berlin,* 1923. 8°.

II. In addition, the following monographs have been devoted to the publication of separate manuscripts:

Sir Thomas Arnold : The Miniatures in Hilāli's mystical poem, The King and the Dervish [at Stockholm]. *Vienna,* 1926. 8°.

F. R. Martin and Sir T. Arnold : The Nizami MS. . . . in the British Museum (Or. 6810). *Vienna, 1926. 8°.*

*Laurence Binyon : The Poems of Nizami [British Museum MS. Or. 2265]. *London, 1928.* Fol.

*Sir T. Arnold : Bihzād and his Paintings in the Zafarnāmah MS. [in the Robert Garrett collection]. *London, 1930. 8°.*

III. For elucidating the various problems, with which from their titles they may be seen to deal, the following books are particularly valuable :

C. Huart : Les Calligraphes et les miniaturistes de l'orient musulman. *Paris, 1908. 8°.*

Sir Thomas Arnold : Survivals of Sasanian and Manichean Art in Persian Painting. *Oxford, 1924. 8°.*

Sir Thomas Arnold : Painting in Islam: a study of the place of pictorial art in Muslim culture. *Oxford, 1928. 4°.*

G. Soulier : Les Influences orientales dans la peinture toscane. *1924. 8°.*

J. M. Upton : Notes on Persian Costumes of the sixteenth and seventeenth centuries. In *Metropolitan Museum Studies,* Vol. II, Pt. 2. *New York, 1930. 4°.*

IV. *General.*

No better introduction to Persian culture can be imagined than the late *Edward G. Browne's* " A Year amongst the Persians . . . 1887–8." (New edition. *Cambridge,* 1926. 8°.) The history of this culture may be followed in detail in the same author's four-volume " Literary History of Persia." (*Cambridge,* 1928. 8°.)

A short treatment of the whole of Persian art is given in *G. Migeon :* " Manuel d'art musulman," 2e édition (2 vols. *Paris,* 1927. 8°); and well illustrated in *H. Glück and E. Diez :* Die Kunst des Islam. (*Berlin,* 1925. 4°.)

* In colour.

PRINTED IN GREAT BRITAIN BY RICHARD CLAY & SONS LIMITED
Bungay, Suffolk